General Health and Safety Tips, A-Z . . . in the African Perspective

General Health and Safety Tips, A-Z . . . in the African Perspective

Olufunmilayo Obisesan-Fajemiseye
TechIOSH SIIRSM MSM AIEHF

To order additional copies of this book, contact:
Xlibris Corporation
0-800-644-6988
www.XlibrisPublishing.co.uk
Orders@XlibrisPublishing.co.uk
302271

Contents

Foreword

Most of the issues discussed in this book are not expected to be entirely new to most of its readers. But it is discussed just to increase people's awareness of things that we often don't pay so much attention to and which may result in dangerous, sometimes very dangerous, situations for people. Hopefully, after reading this book, people will get more awareness about their general and occupational health and safety.

Acknowledgement

My thanks goes first to the Lord God Almighty.

Then to my dear husband, who was of great support throughout the period of writing this book.

To my lovely children, who, I believe, supported my dream and enjoyed themselves in whatever activity they were doing while I wrote the book without any disturbances (as though they knew that mummy was so passionate about this book).

My appreciation also goes to my dear parents, Mr and Mrs D. O. O. Obisesan (I give them the award for the best parents) for denying themselves some of their pleasures to invest for me and for my future.

To my lovely siblings—they are always my strength. There is a saying that 'our friends are our choices but our siblings are by biological chance,' but as for me, apart from we being joined together by the biological chance, if I am to choose, I would have also chosen them to be my friends. They are my dear friends.

The founders of Open Clip Art Library, Jon Phillps and Bryce Harrington, and all who have contributed to the project.

Disclaimer

Efforts have been made to ensure that the information and recommendations in this publication represent the best current opinions on the subjects
discussed at an acceptable safety level. However, other or further measures
may be required depending on individual circumstances. In such cases
a health and safety advice must be sought from a qualified person, and
the author will not assume responsibility therewith.

The author has made effort to trace copyright, the publisher apologises
any unintentional omissions and will be pleased to make any required
acknowledgement in the future editions.

No part of this publication may be reproduced in whole or part or in any
manner without the prior written consent of the author or the publisher.

A—Accidents

Ideally, everybody wishes and hopes to carry on with life and everyday activities with no hitch at all; however, it is always worth preparing for the unexpected because anything can happen at any time.

When most hear the word *accident*, the immediate thought that seems to travel in our mind is of a car crashing into another car, but it is not necessarily so. An accident can be described as an occurrence that was not predicted and which results in harm or damage to property or life. And this may happen anywhere—at home, in religious places of worship, at work, at school, in recreational places, at eateries, etc.

Discussing accidents in detail would possibly require a whole book on its own; this is because there are so many aspects of accidents. But the common thing about all forms of accidents is that it may result in people being injured—temporary or permanent, physical deformities, death, or damage to or loss of property.

There are (and not limited to)

- road accidents—accidents that happen on the road. This may possibly involve head-on-collisions of vehicles or vehicle hitting a pedestrian or object, etc.

- home accidents—accidents that are domestic. Most medical statistics surprisingly show that most accidents occur at home, especially in the kitchens.
- school accidents—accidents that occur in an educational establishment.
- workplace accidents—accidents that occur at a place of work, be it a private establishment, government parastatals or ministry, religious workplace, farm work, etc.

It is, therefore, advisable that you find out and make sure you know the phone numbers of accident-related agencies in operation in your country or state of residence, to contact in cases of emergencies. It has been observed that most people do not even know what numbers to call for help in case of any emergency such as a road accident, fire, flood, etc.

- For Nigeria: You may check the Nigeria police force web site to know the phone number of the police state command for where you reside (http://www.npf.gov.ng). Emergency contact phone number for FRSC is 0700-22553772 and emergency text only number for FRSC is 0807-7690362 (www.frsc.gov.ng).
- For Ghana: The emergency number to dial in an emergency from your house phone or mobile phone is 191 and from TIGO it is 0277522288. You may check the Ghana police Web site for more details on these numbers or any other police-related details. (http://www.ghanapolice.info).

It is always advisable that if you are going to be away from your current place of residence for a period of time, before you leave find out the emergency phone numbers for the place you would be going into. This is because throughout your period of stay away from your country of usual residence, whatever happens to you, especially, emergency situations, will be handled at the place you are at the time of occurrence.

- Before you travel away from your country of residence or immediately you arrive at the country of your destination, make sure you go to the information desk at the airport to confirm what the emergency numbers in the country are, so that you know the emergency number to contact, should any emergency situation occur. Please do not leave yourself in a situation that you cannot get accessible help. Remember this is not your own country of residence, and you may not know the nooks and cranny of this place.

Some people do not have the phone number of their hospital. It is best practice to have the phone number of the hospital you used to go on your phone, and make sure all members of the family knows and have it on their phones too. Remember, you may be the person who require a medical help, imagine if you are the only person who need an urgent medical help and no other member of your family is made aware of your doctor or hospital number. This may imply that an immediate medical help may be delayed and this may cost a life.

Most people have diaries but they make a record of their good and bad days or appointments as priority contents. However, the most important page of a diary which most people often leave blank is the personal data page. The personal data page is the page that will help you to be traceable (hopefully not but) should an accident occur. Remember, a person involved in a fatal accident may not be in a position to speak for him or herself. So as the personal data page of your diary hopefully contains your name, your doctor's name and phone number, and a place to write the name of a contact person and telephone number, then your immediate family member may be contacted on your behalf and be notified of the occurrence.

After reading this book, please make sure you do not leave the personal data page of your diary blank anymore (you may leave any other sensitive information blank as long as the basic necessary information has been made available).

As a backup, it is also advisable to keep a record of this important information on your mobile phone as this may sometimes be handy or readily available, but make sure you use plain words to save the numbers of your phone. For example, *Pale*—popularly used by the Yoruba people in Nigeria to represent Daddy—may not be clear to somebody who is not a Nigerian and who may wish to help you contact your family but does not understand your language or the abbreviation or slang that you have used on your phone; simply save it as *daddy or my dad*.

Remember to have your doctor's number saved in plain language as *my doctor.*

B—Burns

Burn is a kind of injury on the skin. Most time when people hear the word burns, what most often goes in their minds is burns from heat or fire; these are correct, but one can also sustain burns from chemicals, electricity, friction, etc. Burns is one of the most painful injuries that anybody can endure. It may result in tissue damage. There is always a risk of infection during the treatment period, and worst still, in most cases, it leaves a scar and sometimes a permanent scar.

As earlier discussed, electrical shock or fire may result in burns; some caustic chemicals may also cause burns. The immediate treatment for any skin burns is to run under cold water, ideally cool; do not use ointments and seek medical help afterwards.

Boiling water is the most common cause for a scald, which is another form of burns in most homes, especially, where there are young children. The burns suffered from scalding results from the moist heat, which is otherwise called steam.

C—Carbon Monoxide

Carbon monoxide gas is invisible with no smell, this makes it very difficult to detect. But this gas is poisonous and can kill very quickly or cause a serious harm if inhaled over a long period of time. Fumes that come from lanterns, generators, car exhaust, and coal have the potential to contain significant amount of carbon monoxide.

Due to some possible instability in the electricity supply, most houses now have a generator as a substitute to serve this purpose, but generators need to be used as safely as possible by first ensuring that it is located where its fumes can escape into the air properly.

There had been news of people died overnight due to their generator being located close to the bedroom they slept-in and being used overnight (this may be traced to their possible inhaling of carbon monoxide gas from the generator exhaust all through the night).

If you particularly use a generator, the advice therefore is that you should buy a carbon monoxide alarm. It has a sensor that senses the presence of carbon monoxide gas, alarms, and you could escape for your life.

Headaches, dizziness, pain in the chest, and vomiting are some of the signs of a possible carbon-monoxide poisoning. (To buy a carbon monoxide alarm, contact fudemfajnigltd@ymail.com.)

C—Childproof Your House

Every adult and every parent has the responsibility to ensure that the environment is safe for the children by making sure the objects that can cause danger to the children are removed. Children are beautiful gifts. The children, especially crawling babies, do not know that there is anything called danger or possibly they do not have a complete understanding of danger and dangerous things.

Anything that comes out their way appears to them like another exciting toy to be played with, even the things which may be very dangerous to their health and life. This is the most important reason why parents need to ensure that the house is always safe as possible. There are lots of sections of the house that must be child-proofed; below (although not limited to) is a list.

Electrical sockets: The crawling babies and children sometimes find it exciting to put their finger in the socket. Boys tend to be interested in knowing what is inside the socket and will begin to put a metal object in the socket; this may conduct electricity and cause electrical shock (or electrocution). But this can be prevented by buying and putting an electrical sockets-plug guards; this helps to create a sort of inaccessibility to the socket and reduce the possible danger.

Cushion corners: The edges of table could be really dangerous for children if they hit their head on it. Especially, glass table is potentially very dangerous and not recommended for homes with babies and young children; wooden or aluminium tables are seemed to be preferred. However, the four edges of any type of table could be very dangerous; therefore, it is recommended that cushion corners be fixed at the edge. The corner edges are easy to fix and remove by anyone; it doesn't require any carpentry role.

Door stoppers: The danger a door that slams on the hand of any child could be serious. The door stopper helps to ensure that these dangers are minimised or not happening at all. It is advisable that the door stopper is fixed at a height the children cannot reach because it is removable.

Drawer or cupboard latches: These also serve the same purpose similar to that of the door stoppers except that it is designed in such a way that they are applicable for drawers, cabinets, and cupboards.

Cable tidy: This helps to put cables in a tidy way to ensure that one does not mistakenly put hands into a wrong cable and hence reduces the risk of electrical shock. Have a look behind your TV stand and you would see the need to tidy up the untidy.

D—Dangerous Substances

Anything, whether it is in liquid form, gaseous form, or in a solid form that poses a risk to its users when used can be regarded as a dangerous substance.

The awareness about how to control substances that are hazardous or dangerous to health is still a bit low, especially, regarding domestic purposes. Most people usually assume that COSHH—Control of Substances' Hazardous to Health—relates only to big companies and for industrial purposes only; but on the contrary, quite a lot of chemicals are used in the homes too. For example, izal, bleach, jik, even hair perm or hair relaxer that ladies use to retouch the hair, etc. could be hazardous.

These substances, although effectively serve their specific purposes, they could be very dangerous if not handled properly. Therefore, similar advices and precautions as applicable on COSHH in an industrial setting are applicable in handling similar substances in home except that it may not be as comprehensive.

- Always make sure you do not change the container of any chemical (people often have the habit of decanting chemicals, especially into bottles of drinks) so that anybody who comes into contact or handles this chemical could have access to the manufacturer's instruction on the safe handling or usage of this substance.

- Always store chemicals in an upright position (in their original container). This is to avoid possible leaks, as some substances could irritate the skin. Little children could think it is something that can be sipped and such substance may burn their tongue if not poisonous.

- It is always advisable to wear protection on our hands and on our body when using any dangerous substance. Some examples of such required protections are aprons or gloves; as required depending on the substances about to be handled. For example, most hairdressers need to wear gloves to protect their hands when relaxing ladies hair, but is not always the common practice in saloons.

- If you have children in the house, it is always recommended that chemicals, toilet cleaners, relaxer, etc. are stored at a height that children cannot reach. This will help reduce the possibility of children being able to access such chemicals and also the substance becoming a potential poison when swallowed by the children.

E—Escape Plans

It may be weird and particularly scary to start thinking that a fire or something of an emergency could happen to us for real, to an individual or a family or in our houses. But as much as we always hope nothing bad happens to us, it is also a good idea to be realistic and have some sorts of plan, because this plan may save our life should, for example, a fire occurs.

Having an escape plan is worth it, because you want to be sure that your family members know what to do and how to escape should an emergency occurs in the house. And as earlier stated, it could save your life, because instead of being trapped in a fire or smoke from a fire, there will be a ready plan of how to escape from the building, and one is not caught unprepared.

The advice here is to take time, take a walk around your house. While having this walk around your house, think of the possible ways that you can use to safely escape from your house should a fire occurs. Let every member of the household be aware of the escape plan as it makes sense this way. Possibly, take time to practice this plan together to make sure that everybody knows what to do.

Another suggestion for anyone who is just about to build a house is this: ensure that there are enough exits in the building, i.e., a front and a back door. Having just one main door in a building is not very advisable. Using the example of a fire, as earlier stated in this section, think about a situation when a fire occurs in your house and you and your entire household need to escape, reaching the only way or the only exit door would require going through the fire since there is no alternative door. This is dangerous, and the person may catch fire or inhale smoke; too much smoke inhaled is also very dangerous.

This danger could simply be avoided if there is an alternative exit door and a planned and communicated escape plan.

(If you invite *fudemfajniglt* to conduct a home safety check for your house, the report will give suggestions as regarding possible escape plan as unique to your building. Contact via fudemfajnigltd@ymail.com.)

F—Fire

Fire needs three things to start: first, air or oxygen, which is normally readily available; second, fuel, and fuel in this case does not necessarily have to be fuel as in petrol, for example, uncleaned accumulated oil on a cooker is a potential fuel; and third, the combustible material; the combustible material is anything that has the potential to catch fire, and this can be anything, for example, piece of paper, clothes, etc.

National and international records reflect that most fires occur at homes. This is because of the way we handle the things we use at home, such as candles and electrical appliances and also because of the kitchen activities.

This section will not deal with the kitchen activities as there is a section where this is looked in detail.

An overloaded socket apart from the fact that it could cause an electric shock has a possibility of causing an electrical spark and hence a possible fire. To avoid overloading, which may cause an electrical fire, buy a conjunction box but please ensure that the conjuction box is not overloaded.

In individual case, each person's house is different in terms of level of good housekeeping and house layout. It is a little difficult going into many details in this section, but the general recommendation which will be applicable to any house is given in the example below.

- Locating a basket full of dirty clothes, ready for washing, close to the cooking area maybe a fire waiting to happen. The clothes in the laundry basket as the fuel or combustible material, naked fire from the cooking area as ignition, and oxygen, which is readily available makes all three necessary components to start a fire.
- When trying to switch to generator supply of electricity, possibly due to erratic power supply or low voltage, it is good idea to have a torchlight readily available to access where the house generator is located. The common practice by people is going into the generator house or location with a lantern. This can be dangerous because there is naked light in the lantern, and remember that the air is always readily available, should there be any spill of petrol in the generator house, and this may be a fire waiting to happen.
- In companies and corporate environment, it is a statutory responsibility to have fire extinguishers for fire safety purposes. Also, anyplace where a fire could happen needs to have a fire extinguisher, and the people there must be able to use it; otherwise it will be as good as not having one at all. However, it is very important to use the right fire extinguisher for the right purpose, so that one who is using it will not make the fire worse; this is

because some extinguishers can only be used for some specific causes, for example, some can be used only on electrical items.

- (If you invite *fudemfajnigltd* via fudemfajnigltd@ymail.com to conduct a home safety check for your house, the report will give suggestions as regarding possible things that may cause fire in your building and recommend the appropriate safety solutions.)

F—First Aid

Just like the title implies aid means assistance and first means initial. First aid could, therefore, be described as the initial form of assistance a person gets before a medical help arrives or is sought. Anybody trained in the administration of first aid can administer first aid, the person does not have to be a medically trained personnel to be trained in the administration of first-aid. Ideally, it is the best idea that everybody in a household—parents and each child—be trained in the administration of first aid. You never know who will be left with you in an emergency and you may need first aid as the saving grace for your life. For example, non-stop bleeding may lead to death if there is no first-aid-kit or in a situation where the person around does not know how to administer the contents of the first-aid-kit as applicable to the situation on ground. It will be as bad as not having a first-aid-kit at all, for example, like using the bandage to stop or reduce the bleeding before a medical help arrives.

Emergency situation that may require the administration of first aid may happen at any place. It may happen in schools, religious houses, restaurants and canteens, offices, on the road or in the car, in the house, etc. This is the reason why there must be a first-aid-kit for each location. The contents of each first-aid-kit may differ based on the possible emergency occurrences that may occur in each place. For example, the contents of a car first-aid-kit may be similar but will differ as applicable to possible occurrence in the car compared to a home first-aid-kit or a school first-aid-kit.

Parents are advised to get trained in the administration of *baby and child first aid*. Some parents, because they do not know what to do, watch their child die before medical help arrives. Administration of first aid on anybody may be the thin line between his life and death.

Car first-aid-kit has been proved to be very helpful for emergency cases, especially, before medical help arrives. Imagine an emergency occurrence on an expressway, where hospitals are not nearby, some of the items in the first-aid-kit can found to be very useful until medical help is sought.

G—Guarding

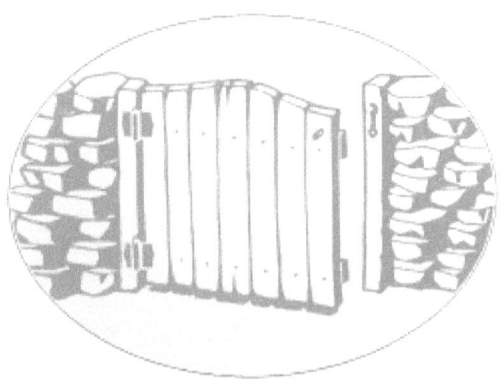

Guarding should be a priority action, especially for parents with grow-ing children just similar to childproofing the house (especially with crawling babies). Babies and toddlers are in the highest risk of getting injured at home; this is because they have not yet fully understood the concept of danger. Interestingly, things that pose some serious danger usually appear exciting to children hence they wish to explore it. It appears like another toy for them to play with, for example, a flame from a burning candle can surprisingly be exciting to children and they may want to touch.

This is the reason why it is important to guard our house properly, as even the most watchful parent cannot keep their children completely from harm all day and every day.

It might be very worthwhile to put a guard on the stairs should your house be a duplex (to prevent children falling off from the stairs, especially the crawling babies) and a guard on your kitchen door to monitor and control unsupervised children access, especially when there may be hot or cooking food, flame from stove, or gas cooker.

Another way to guard our houses from unauthorised entry is to fix anti-burglary locks into the windows and appropriate locks on the door. Leaving the gate of your house visibly open by not locking with key or padlock is like indirectly saying that anybody is welcome. (Contact fudemfajnigltd@ymail.com to purchase the recommended house-guarding hardware.)

H—Hand Washing

Effective hand washing is the first defence action against the spread of infections. Hand washing, like it sounds, is the washing and cleaning of hands. This could be by using water or where water is not available, by other suitable measures, for example, hand cleaning gel.

However, it has been observed through surveys that most people do not wash their hands after using the toilet, especially if the person has gone only to wee and not to pooh. People tend to think that not washing hands after a wee is not as bad as not washing hands after a pooh. The fact in both the scenarios is that you have just used the toilet, and the toilet seat or toilet accessories, depending on the level of hygiene and where they are located, may contain some invisible micro-organisms. These may come in contact with our hands while using the toilet, which is the main reason that irrespective of what we have gone to do in the toilet, hands must be washed after using the toilet (take a minute to sincerely reflect. Do you always wash your hands every time you use the toilet?). Most people wash hands after using their hands to eat, obviously to wash off the food items or stains on their hands, especially if it is an oily food (Please take another minute; this time, again, be honest. Do you always wash your hands before eating every of your meal?). Most time people just dust their two hands, blow it, and start to eat.

How many mothers wash their hands after changing their baby's nappy or diaper? Most mums just carry on with the next activity, which may likely be preparing the baby's meal. Imagine that scenario—the hands that have just been used to clean up a baby's pooh, for example, and then used straight to prepare the baby's meal. Remember, that most disease-causing micro-organism and bacteria are invisible, so it is important to always ensure that hands are properly washed after handling a baby's nappy before going on with the next activity even if the next activity is not making the baby's meal, as this will imbibe in individuals. The habit of hand washing is the first defence against the spread of infections.

Many medical seminars and journals have proved that the most important and effective way of preventing the spread of infection carriers (pathogens) is by effective hand washing.

Hand washing with soap and water is okay, but if hands are needed to be washed where there is no water, for example, while driving along expressway, then the use of alcohol gel hand rub could serve the purpose of hand wash (please note, if you have just finished eating, your hands may need to be properly cleaned with, maybe, tissue paper, before applying the hand rub).

(Order portable hand-cleaning gel, which you can always carry in your handbag and use anytime you need to wash your hands where there is no soap and water.)

Another point to note regarding hand washing is that on many occasions, we wash our hands but not properly. Some people just run water over their hands. This is as good as not washing their hands at all.

The following are the recommended ways of effective hand washing:

- Palm to palm wash
- Right palm over left and vice versa
- Palm to palm with fingers interlocked
- Backs of fingers to opposing palms
- Rotational rubbing of right thumb clasped in left palm and vice versa

(www.nhs.co.uk/handwashing)

Listing these hand-washing steps is not to scare anybody; it really will not take more than two to three minutes, and it is just to give us an idea of the areas that must be washed to ensure an effective hand wash.

Please cultivate the habit of effective hand washing and make sure that your children emulate this idea too. It is the most effective way to control the spread of infectious diseases, especially diarrhoea, vomiting, and respiratory diseases.

Hand washing is also very important after touching a pet. Most people in Africa raise their own chicken, dogs, or goats in their garden for using them during the festive periods. After been to the pet house to feed or clean the house, the hands should be properly washed, if not, some micro-organism, which may cause disease, might get attached to you, in doing so. The recommendation is to ensure hands are effectively washed and, preferably, done outside before entering into house again so that these possible, diseases causing micro-organisms have not been carried into the house.

(Pictorial explanation of effective hand wash can be ordered from fudem-fajnigltd@ymail.com for display in your school toilets, cafeteria toilets, church or mosque toilets, and recreation centre's toilets.

Are you a proprietor of a nursery or a primary or a secondary school? Would you like us to supply you with school resources to teach or educate your pupils on effective hand washing methods through exciting teaching modes such as games, videos? Would you also want your pupils to register and participate in Global Hand Washing Day, then please contact us on fudemfajnigltd@ymail.com).

H—Healthy Eating Habits

Most African people tend to have their plates always full. It is the common style among Africans. The objective is always to have the stomach full, but eating should be more than just having a full stomach. The objective should be we have to ensure that the body receives as much nourishment as possible through our food intake. Most of the time, the food combination is just too starchy. The dieticians recommend that more colourful the contents in our plate are, more likely our meal is healthy.

Most African youths are now cultivating the habit of eating what is popularly called as junk meals or unhealthy meals because of the laziness to cook. A lot of junk meals means too much of fat, or too much salt or sugar content and that is not good for the body.

Most of our youthful habits always have their effect on our bodies when we get old, including our eating habit. It, therefore, makes sense to begin to look after the body from now on by making sure that what we eat from now on are healthy and nourishing to the body.

Pastries and sugary snacks: Some busy people, especially people who work in corporate organisations, tend to get too busy to nourish their body with good healthy meals that they tend to feed on pastries and sugary snacks almost every day. The advice is to cultivate the habit of eating fruits instead of pastries. There are some fruits that make us feel full as though we have eaten a full meal, for example, apple, which is a healthy snack option compared to pastries. It is, therefore, recommended that fruits like apple can be eaten in place of pastries and sugary snacks while we are at work and feel hungry. And it is advisable to find a chance to eat a healthy and nourishing meal.

Surveys have shown that most working-class people, compared to people in the rural area, do not eat much fruit. The advice is to eat five fruits a day; so not eating any fruit at all is not good for the body. Some of the fruits are rich in fibre, some are rich in vitamin C, etc. and they give the body a lot of nourishment.

Children and eating of fruits: Parents need to train their children to like eating fruits rather than sweets and chocolates, which seemed to have become the alternative where the reverse should have been the case. Parents should cultivate the habit of making fruits attractive to eat for their children. This can be done by involving them in the preparation of the fruits in an exciting way, especially, by allowing the child to be involved in cutting the fruit (using a safe knife, of course, e.g. plastic knife). Preparing fruit dishes can be fun. For example, making a fruit salad, involving your children may make it more interesting for them than just handing out a particular fruit to them or another fun way would be making a fruit smoothie which children may find easier than crunching.

Another way to make fruit-eating habit as a part of our daily life is to plant at least a fruit-bearing tree in your house. There are lots of varieties of fruit seeds that can be bought from the market and planted in your house. If you have a paw-paw tree in your garden, you will naturally eat from it when it is ripe because it is readily available and it does not go waste; and by doing so the body is also been nourished.

Water drinking: Another healthy habit is to drink water. This appears not to be a common practice amongst us. A lot of people find it easy to buy any other kind of drink like soft drinks, malt drinks, and beers than to buy water to drink. To cultivate the habit of drinking water is very good. Six to eight glasses of water a day is recommended. Water drinking will help us able to get the toilet routine done very easily without having to push hard and also it helps to flush the body system and reduces the risk of kidney problems, ensuring that the body is well hydrated is good for the human brain.

I—Ironing

Careless domestic ironing often causes the highest percentage of paediatric burns with some posing serious injuries or scars.

Most adults, after finished ironing their clothes, tend to forget the action priorities. The common action by some people is to first take the ironed clothes away to where it will not get crumpled again or stained; possibly to put on a cloth hanger in the wardrobe when the reverse is the recommended safety action which is to put away the hot iron where nobody else can mistakenly run into this hot iron and get burns. Other activities such as hanging the clothes in the wardrobe may follow afterwards. This should always be the case especially where there are children around, particularly crawling babies, to reduce the risk of iron burns.

Another common habit but that is very dangerous because it could pose the risk of an electrical shock is cleaning the face of the stained iron while in use. Most people do not bother to switch off and unplug the iron before cleaning the face; this is very dangerous. Always ensure that the iron is switched off and unplugged before carrying out a face-cleaning activity on a hot iron so that it reduces the risk of an electrical shock.

Most people use their iron by inserting bare wires into the socket (possibly because the plug is broken). Our life is worth more than the price of a plug. So buy a plug for this purpose to ensure that there is no loop hole for a possible electric shock. Some cables of irons might have cuts; depending on the level of damage, this may simply be needed to be covered by insulation tape or may require buying a new iron. Again, our lives are worth more than the price of an iron.

If you use a steam iron, be careful of the evaporating steam Do not put your face directly to where the steam is coming as this may cause scalding.

It is also advisable that iron should be stored at a height that children cannot reach and of course, with the face of the iron facing inside, especially if it has just been used and is still hot.

J—Just Keep It Safe

List of things to keep safe is endless, but in this section, the attention is given to documents.

There are some documents of utmost value such as academic certificates, birth certificates (possibly yours and your children's birth certificates), and marriage certificate that many people had lost because of house fires.

Photographs of precious moments such as wedding pictures could be lost to fire or by water spills, etc. if not kept safely.

The first recommendation is that some of this document can be made safer by laminating or being kept in waterproof document folders. For example, a laminated document is protected from an accidental tear or a possible damage from water spill. Please note that it could still be vulnerable to fire.

The ideal way to keep these valuables is to have a *safety box* in your home. Most safety boxes are fire and flood resistant (i.e. fire and water-proof). To think of the stress involved in getting replacement for burnt academic certificate makes it more reasonable to purchase a safety box for your household. Unfortunately, there are some documents which cannot be replaced, for example, some wedding photos that were taken when technology had not developed so much and digital cameras were not very popular. These are precious memories and it could be very pain-ful to lose. Hopefully not, but should a house fire or flooding occurs, if these precious documents and items are stored in the safety box, you can be sure that your documents are safe.

(Contact fudemfajnigltd@ymail.com to buy yours.)

K—Kitchen Safety

Most fires at homes start in the kitchen. Things that are often taken for granted cause such fires, e.g. *domestic gas.* Not remembering to properly turn off the valve of the gas cylinder could cause gas leaks and may ignite with any small naked lights, e.g. a lantern brought near or someone using a lit matchstick close by. It is also advisable to place your gas cylinder where children cannot reach the gas knob; otherwise, a gas knob or valve may appear like another toy that could be played with (this is very important; remember, your eyes cannot be everywhere, so doing the right thing always saves a lot. It could save properties from getting damaged or lost, and more importantly, it saves life).

Stove: Some stoves might be leaking and they might have been placed in a tray to collect the leaking kerosene while it is continued to be used for cooking. This is really dangerous because a possible explosion may occur, especially if such a leaking stove is used with adulterated kerosene, that is sometimes smuggled into the market for sale to innocent consumers. Life is worth more than the cost of a new stove even if it means buying a cheap brand (a cheap brand is, of course, better than a leaking cooking stove; think of a possible explosion that may happen, especially, due to adulterated kerosene, as illustrated above).

Deep fryer or oven: These kitchen appliances are good; just a lot of kitchen activities are done very quickly, compared to the traditional methods of doing them. But these kitchen appliances do accumulate grease over continuous use. Accumulated grease can be categorised as fuel and oxygen is always around, so when you ignite your oven to use it, then the three components necessary to start a fire are present, and all you have just done is having started a fire.

Clean your kitchen appliances regularly to be free of grease or oil; remember, as long as one necessary component is missing, a fire will not start.

Sandwich maker or toaster: It is advisable not to allow bread crumbs to get accumulated in your toaster because accumulated crumbs could be categorised as fuel, which could support a fire to start in a toaster that is hot (which could ignite), and remember that oxygen is always around.

Electrical safety in the kitchen: It is not safe to use any electrical appliance with an open cable (it is just not worth taking the risk). So if any kitchen appliance, such as kettle, deep fryer, fridge, electric cooker, and so on, has an open or cut cable, please discontinue using it. You might have been risking, using it for a long time and nothing serious had happened, but the unfortunate story is that this faulty cable appliance will not give you a notice of the day when a danger may occur.

It is also advisable to subject your kitchen appliances to a PAT as most of the kitchen electrical items will fall in the category of portable appliance. And by doing so, it will give you more peace of mind that the probability of your appliance resulting in anything dangerous is low.

Footwear in the kitchen: It is always advisable to wear slippers while in the kitchen, especially while touching a fridge or freezer, to avoid electrical shocks. Electrical appliances with damaged cable when exposed to water can cause electrical shocks or electrocution. Also, when taking frozen stuffs out of the fridge or freezer, do not use a knife to get this done; ideally, switch off the fridge or freezer and use a hard plastic or wooden (not metal) spoon to get your stuff out. This could save you from shock.

Hot oil: Most African dishes involve heating up the oil before the proper cooking begins if the hot oil starts to smoke, remove it from the heat (stove or cooker) to cool for a while before continuing with the cooking, otherwise it could catch fire.

Also, if you have to leave the cooking oil unattended at any time, the advice is that you put off the stove or cooker because the unexpected might happen before you return.

Use fridge and freezer thermometers: Most homes do not have a thermometer for the fridge and freezer. There are a lot of effective and cheap brands of thermometers in the market. The thermometers are very good to help ensure that our frozen and chilled items are stored in the correct temperature so that the risk of food poisoning can be avoided. Ideally, the fridge should be below 5°C and freezer should be below 18°C or slightly below, at these temperatures, bacteria cannot grow.

Washing of food items: Some farm produce may look like it has been washed already, when we buy it from the market. But the advice is to always make sure that you personally wash any food items such as vegetables and fruits again before cooking or eating. Although the vegetable or fruit might have been washed before it has been displayed for sale, you need to think about how many people have possibly held such food items all day before you eventually bought it. And since you cannot vouch for another person's level of hygiene and do not know what they have done with their hands before touching just to know the price of such food items, without eventually buying them. It is therefore advisable, for your own safety, to ensure that all such food items are rewashed before use or before eating, to avoid the possible diseases these may cause.

Boiling ring: Most people, especially students, tend to use the boiling ring to cook food, especially food like beans, which people tend to avoid using their stove or cooker to cook because it takes comparatively a longer time to cook and thus deciding to use the boiling ring. The first recommendation is that there is a serious danger in using an electrical appliance for a purpose which it was not manufactured for. An electrical appliance has a specification for which it was designed and not for the kind of activities you try doing with the appliance. The manufacturer would have carried out a quality control test on such appliance before launching it into the market for sale. Unfortunately, although such an electrical appliance would work very efficiently when put to the right use, as recommended by its manufacturer, it will malfunction, if not cause a danger, when it is used for purposes other than it has been designed for.

Microwave oven: It makes our food hot at the click of the button on the wall without going through the stress of setting up the stove or cooking gas, and by doing so, it tends to be the quicker, perhaps an easy, method in getting work done. It is very important to ensure that the food being warmed in the microwave is warmed using the correct plate. Some plates, especially most plastic plates, are not designed to be put in the microwave as the heat from the microwave will melt this plate and possibly cause fire. Always check the bottom of the plate to be sure that whether it is safe for using it in the microwave. This is because most manufacturers write under or beside on most plates advising their customer whether the plate is safe or not to be used in the microwave. It is also good to get the food on the right temperature for warming and such temperature should be based on the quantity. Quite often, people set too much time compared to the quantity of the food being warmed in the microwave, and will leave the microwave unattended after putting the food in it, thus leaving the food to be warmed, dried, burnt, and may possibly catch fire. Some food has the recommended microwave time written on its label. It is advisable that this time be followed. In situations where there are no recommended microwave times, it is advisable to try from very small period of time and gradually increase it as and when required until the food is satisfactorily warmed.

Some people use the microwave to actually cook food, for example to cook rice. Technology is improving everyday, except a microwave has been designed to carry out such activity, that the microwave was able to cook the rice does not justify the continuous use of the microwave for cooking rice (as an example). It is very important to ensure that an electrical item is used solely for the purposes that its manufacturer says it can serve to avoid any unforeseeable danger.

There are a lot of worrying questions that had been asked about how safe or unsafe the use of microwave is and where and when it is best to warm food using the stove or cooker.

It is also advisable that each kitchen should have a fire extinguisher and a fire blanket that is readily available for use should a fire needs to be quenched because kitchen is the most vulnerable part of the house. It is good to have fire extinguishers on other parts of the house also. And everybody in the house needs to be able to use it; otherwise it will be as good as not having any.

Food storage in the kitchen store: Apart from the fact that it is very important to ensure that our food items are well covered where they are stored, it is also very important to ensure that they are stored in such a way that we will not be in a risk of a back sprain or injury when trying to access these food items. The advice, therefore, is to always store the heavier food items on the lower shelves where any lifting may not even be necessary in the course of accessing it. The lighter food items can be stored on the higher shelves, and this will reduce the necessity for anybody trying to access these food items from leaning forward, tip-toeing to reach, which may result in a fall due to unbalanced standing position or back strain. In a corporate setting, where manual handling and lifting is a part of work activities, the staff should be sent on the safe-manual-handling course which teaches the correct postures to be adopted for any manual handling and lifting activity.

L—Lanterns

Lanterns are used to give an immediate illumination when the daylight is over or electricity is not available at the time. Lanterns are to be used safely, similar to leaking stove which were explained in the last section. Leaking lanterns are never to be placed in a tray for collecting the leaking kerosene and be lit for vision or illumination. It is dangerous; it could catch fire. Remember, naked light is on in the lantern, oxygen is around, just one more thing, and a fire may start.

A lantern whose globe is not clean may not give an adequate illumination; continuous use of such lantern with an unclean shade (especially by students for studying) may cause eye problem. To wash the shade of your lantern, sparkle clean it before lighting it. Ideally it will not take more than five minutes, but most times this is done in so much hurry that after the shade had been cleaned, it did not have much difference from what it was before the cleaning.

M—Motor Cars

Motor car is a form of transport that is widely relied on for movement from one place to another. In our cars, we carry various people, our families, and friends, including you as the driver of the car. It is, therefore, worth ensuring that your motor car is well cared for as lives are always entrusted into it when put on the road to get to our desired destinations.

Daily checks are often taken for granted by most car owners and drivers, but if we recall that we do entrust our lives into this car, then when up and about we should make this recommended daily check as a priority action everyday. It is advised, before moving the car everyday, to carry out a simple visual all-round check. This check will not take so much time, especially, if the car is in good condition.

Below is a list (not limited to) of some recommended everyday visual car check:

- Check your brake, brake light, and brake oil.
- Gauge your engine oil.
- Check water level and washer.
- Check headlight and traffic-indicator.
- Check tyre pressure to ensure correct pressure gauge in your tyre (this will protect you against tyre burst).

MOT is advisable, most cars in Africa have MOT certificate without actually undergoing or passed a MOT test. The interesting part of this kind of action is that, such MOT certificate may make your car escape a law enforcing officer from charging you of any related offence but at the end of the day, you know that the MOT was never done, and you will be entrusting lives of your loved ones and yourself into this car when driving it. It is, therefore, gives you a peace of mind if you truly take your car for a MOT test because you can be sure that it is road worthy, which is the whole essence of been asked by the traffic enforcement bodies to do MOT test.

It is economically wise for the car owner to take his car for the MOT test, as faults in the car can be identified early during the MOT test will help to prevent further damages in the car, and in the long run will lead to a possible increase in the lifespan of the car, Also, giving your car a regular service and routine check, for example brake pad check, helps to avoid unnecessary accidents such as brake failure, engine knock, etc, and more importantly save your life and avoid physical deformities that accidents might cause. Most people tend to leave the servicing of their car to when they want to embark on a journey. It is a good idea to buy a book and log in any repairs and servicing done on it to ensure a regular and continuous care for your car and be able to track when your brake pad, as an example, was last serviced.

Do you have a fire extinguisher in your car? Do not wait till the enforcement officers (police or FRSC) start to check for them before you buy one for your car; because anything can cause a fire to happen at any time. And ugly situations does not send us a message of when it wants to happen, it is, therefore, reasonable to be prepared so one is not caught unaware, and a fire extinguisher in the car could save yours or somebody's life.

Eye check: This should not be taken for granted. Some people cannot see objects which are too far or too close, very clearly. This means, such a person will not see early enough the possible hazards on the road when he is driving. It is advisable to get to see an optician if you have any concerns about your eyesight. And for everybody, an eye check for every two years is recommended so that they will be able to get early awareness of any deterioration in their eyesight.

For your safety, always ensure that the doors of your car is kept locked when you are in traffic, otherwise known as *hold-up* in African slang, as the highway thieves may take advantage of you to force access to your car if it is not locked. And also when your car is parked, always ensure that the valuable things are stored out of sight, e.g. handbag or laptop, etc. as this may attract potential thieves and the car might be broken into. Whenever possible ensure that your car is parked in a well-lit area, it will further boost its security as a potential thieve will not wish to be seen burgling into the car and might change his or her mind from doing so.

For safety sake, it is wise to embark on any journey early enough, especially journeys to places that we have not been before or we are not very familiar with so that there will not be the pressure of driving too fast to ensure arriving at the destination at the risk of your life. Remember the popular saying, 'It is better late than never.' It is also reasonable to avoid travelling to unfamiliar places at night as people may know from your actions that you are new in the area popularly known in the African slang as JJC—Jolly Just Come and the bad people may take advantage of this.

Also for safety sake, it is important to embark on any journey with enough fuel because there might be a possibility that for the entire journey you will be in the car. To rely on buying more fuel along the way may be risky, as proposed filling station may have run out of fuel or there may be something happening on the way. Not having enough fuel in the car may leave you stranded in the middle of the journey, possibly on the expressways, and you may be left with no choice but to sleep in the car till next day to get more fuel, which is very dangerous. And you may be left with no choice but to buy more fuel at an exorbitant rate.

Car first-aid-kit: It has been proved to be very helpful for emergency cases, especially before medical help arrives. Imagine an emergency occurrence on an expressway, where hospitals are not nearby, some of the items in the first-aid-kit can be found to be very useful until medical help is sought.

(Please contact fudemfajnigltd@ymail.com to order your car first-aid-kit.)

N—Night-Time Checks

Researches has shown that the worst fires are the fires that start at night because as it is usually the case, the person involved may be asleep so there is no immediate alertness or notice of a started fire, but the risk of this could be reduced by cultivating the habit of a night-time check.

A night check is ideally a very quick look around the house to ensure everything is safe. It may include (not limited to) the following

- Ensure that the cooking stove is completely off (sometimes the wick is only turned down and left as such all through the night).
- Ensure that the gas cylinder knob is switched off (sometimes the knob is not properly switched off thereby causing gas leak, and this is an explosion waiting to happen because at a small flame, the fire may start).
- Ensure that the electric cooker is turned off and unplugged (if not properly turned off, an electrical fire may happen).
- Ensure no boiling ring is plugged, obviously to avoid explosion or electrical fire.
- Ensure to blew out all the candles, do not leave it till later because you may get tired and doze off. Remember, the candle is a naked fire and that with anything combustible close by (e.g. paper) and with air or oxygen, which is readily available completes the cycle for a fire to start and hence a fire may start. So do not get caught up in that. Another common issue with candles, which can be a potential danger, is when people stick a lit candle directly in to a surface. For example, some people tend to let the lit candle make some wax and then pour some of the wax on the reading table edge and stick the candle unto it for illumination to read. This can be very dangerous, the wax from the candle can be regarded as fuel itself, the table made from wood is of course a combustible material, and air (oxygen) is always readily available. That is like a fire waiting to happen, especially if there are books close by. The recommendation is that in situations, where a candle has to be used, it has to be stuck on a candle holder. Candle holders have been designed to collect the wax that a candle makes while it has been lit in such a way that it will minimise the potential danger that may happen.
- Ensure to turn off your generator. Due to possible unstable power supply, many people tend to run their generator all through the

night so that they can power their fan or air condition because of heat. This is not a very good idea; it may not be too bad if the generator is located separately from the building, for example in a generator house. But if your situation such that you have your generator just behind your room then it can be dangerous because of the risk of breathing in carbon monoxide through out the night. Please refer to *carbon monoxide* section of this book for details).

Ensure that all the entry doors (or house gate) are locked as this will further boost your security. There may be a possibility that the last person to come into the house may just close the door behind him, without actually locking it up with key. This may not be out of a deliberate nonchalant attitude of this person, it could be that the person rushed in (for example, to use the toilet) but forgetting to lock it up with key. A night time check will help to spot this possible over sight and the right thing could then be done.

In conclusion, anything that does not appear safe is not worth been ignored and any unused electrical appliance should be switched off and unplugged during your night check before going to bed.

O—Observance

Being observant entails (not limited to) keeping an eye out for things that may cause any form of harm; this may be in terms of keeping an eye on our health and on our domestic or outdoor activities. Some people work so hard that they do not make time out to monitor their blood pressure (BP) regularly, and that is why there is an increased number of youthful deaths. Ideally, each household needs to have a blood pressure monitor (there are a lot of cheap and easy-to-read blood pressure monitor). When asked, each person should be able to mention their blood pressure every time (an average of every three days check is recommended).

Some people are diabetic; it is, therefore, reasonable to keep an observant eye on the food they eat and regularly check their blood sugar level as recommended by their doctor. Some people are asthmatic; therefore, it makes sense for them to be aware of any environment they go to. For example, if the asthmatic person is going to a crusade ground where there may be stuffiness or a lot of dust, it is recommended that such person should find a location (on such a crusade ground) that is well ventilated and not so prone to the dust, to stay. This may help the person to avoid an asthmatic attack. And, of course, remember to carry your inhaler with you always.

A good domestic example (among other things) is taking time to evaluate. Evaluating the locations of your jerry-canned petrol, you have kept for the refill of your generator and your kitchen is a good example. Petrol is a highly flammable liquid (i.e. it may catch fire very quickly). If your kitchen is located close to where naked fire is used for cooking (e.g. the kerosene stove or gas cooker) and where air or oxygen is readily available then it is most likely a fire waiting to happen.

It is reasonable to ensure that your house is as safe as possible. Be observant, and at the end of your observation, it may require that some stuffs are needed to be removed, relocated, or completely disposed off.

Extra care should be taken if you have babies or small children in your house. For example, the flame of a burning candle may attract them and it may appear like another toy that should be explored. Babies may crawl towards it to have a feel and eventually get burns. Also, dangerous house substances, as earlier discussed, should be stored high so children and crawling babies cannot reach.

In a corporate setting, there is a statutory obligation to conduct *workplace inspection*. This process involves a qualified health and safety officer inspecting a workplace to observe and identify possible dangerous things (objects or actions), evaluating the level of risk, and make recommendations for appropriate remedial actions. The same (although not as intense) can be done in your house to ensure you are not overlooking some possible dangers in your home.

Some people store household items, for example cutlass, in the general store in the house. This is very dangerous, especially in houses where there are children. Such household items are to be stored under lock. The door handle to such stores are recommended to be kept high enough so that the children cannot reach.

Some kitchen items such as knives are recommended to be kept out of sight. For example, they can be kept in a knife block, located in a cupboard preferably high up as this will protect bare hands from the sharp edges; not only for children but for adults also. There was a story of past, where a woman stabbed her husband with a domestic knife mistakenly because that was the immediate item she could spot when she was at the peak of her anger. Unfortunately, according to this story, the husband died, but the deed which was done is done. So it is always advised that knifes should be located strategically high-up and out of sight in the kitchen.

Parents need to be observant enough to be able to notice a mood change of their child or children (may be due to ill health) in a very short period. At nights, parents should be more observant; this may require waking from sleep to go to the children's room to ensure that they are still sleeping and they are safe too.

Some cars drivers are not very observant with changes occurring in their cars. A lot of car accidents could have been avoided if their owners or drivers were observant enough to notice its early warning signs. For example, in most cases, a car break failure would have given the driver the signs of malfunctioning which should have alerted the driver or owner to take it to the mechanic garage for necessary repairs; but lack of being an observant may leave one to be caught unaware.

(Please contact fudemfajnigltd@ymail.com to purchase a house inspection checklist that you may use when having an informal inspection of your house. This contains the list of basic things—which are usually overlooked—to look out for. If you send your honest checklist back to us, we will be able to advise you accordingly).

P—Potential Poison

There are quite a few orthodox or African improvised solutions which have been used to provide solutions (sometimes short term) to some immediate problems. Most of these improvised solutions undoubtedly work, but they may pose some serious dangers if adequate care is not taken. A good example is the local rat or insect killer. The common usage of rat killer involves buying a rat killer from the market, mixing it with food or sweet-aroma food like fish, and putting it in the corners of our house to attract the rat to eat and get poisoned and die.

Sometimes, some people use indoseed capsules for this purpose. These can be very dangerous. The rat killer bought from the market is not produced by a trained pharmacist, nor is it certified safe for use, by appropriate standards or regulatory offices in charge of such substances.

It is very understandable that rats and insects can be a big nuisance in the house—they feed and contaminate our food, spoil clothes, eat books, etc.

Rat and insect killers may appear to help you kill rats and the insects, which can be described as a short-term solution, but take time to think of the possible dangerous effects that this may leave you with, after the rat or insects have been killed. The first possible thing is this: a dying insect may struggle pass through the area where your foodstuffs are stored. If any of these food items are left uncovered, then there is the possibility of food getting contaminated with the insect droppings, which you may eat and could be possibly poisoned too. The same could be the case of a dying rat also.

Also, here the emphasis is placed on children because of their naivety in recognising a danger or a dangerous thing. Think of another scenario, where a poisoned fish is left as a target to attract a rat, but no rat fed on it till daybreak, and a baby crawling towards it and finds it. Ideally, for most crawling babies, everything they come into contact with goes into their mouth; this means such a baby could be poisoned when it finds the poisoned fish attractive and eats it.

Here are some simplest solutions to rat or insect problems:

- Ensure that your stores are clean. Empty any unnecessary clutters, as these may attract the insects.
- Store your food items in covered plastic containers. Some food items stored in sacks may be eaten by rat. Ensure that your store is well lit; dark areas and shades attract insects and rats.
- Employ the services of *house fumigators,* and your whole house could be fumigated against insects, thereby providing a possible lasting solution to the problem of insects and rats (contact fudemfajnigltd@ymail.com for further advice on this).

The advice here is that you should make sure you employ the right service.

Q—Quality

There is the popular adage that says 'Buy cheap, buy twice'. It is understandable that some quality products are sometimes expensive, and most people sometimes cannot afford to buy them. Having said that, the difference in the price of a quality one and its sub-standard imitation is definitely not worth the risk that may be entailed in buying the sub-standard one, especially with electrical items.

People often reject the quality electrical item (which has the manufacturer's warranty) to buy the sub-standard imitation. The risk in this is enormous, apart from the fact that such an electrical item is not very reliable and can break down quite quickly than expected, which obviously means that a replacement should be purchased. If this item was a quality item and breaks down, then it may be repaired for free by the manufacturer, or a replacement will be given if it is still within the warranty period.

Increased electrical waste is also not good for the environment.

Examples in terms of quality are not limited to electrical items. The general recommendation here is that an imitation can never be better than the original.

Interestingly, most mechanics do advise the car owners to buy a fairly used imported spare part also known as *tokubo spare part* saying its original counterpart does not last as this. Please take a minute to think on what could be the reason where this *tokubo-part* was dumped by its primary owner. Obviously, it was because something might be wrong. Why will you then believe that something that someone has removed from his car—because of a problem, which you do not know—would be safe for you to use in your own car.

Most mechanics give this advice because *tokubo spare parts* are sometimes cheaper compared to a new part, and it will solve that problem in your car only for a short while so that you will come back to fix it soon; this keeps them in business. Remember, you entrust your life and the lives of your loved ones in your car when you drive it, so, please, always insist to use original or new parts for your car.

Another simple way to identify if an item you are about to spend your money on is truly of good quality is to check for quality certification number or stamp of the appropriate standards organisation or the appropriate regulatory body in your country that is in charge of regulating or certifying that substance you are thinking of buying and using for example "The Standard Organisation of Nigeria—SON and NAFDAC" etc. This quality seal or number will further give you the confidence that you are buying quality.

R—Risky

To try to make a list of risky things could be an endless process, but here the focus is given to things that are commonly risky in home:

- Smoking in a bed is very dangerous; the bed sheet may catch fire especially if the cigarette is not properly put out.

- Not blowing out a candle could be as dangerous as smoking in bed for similar reasons.

- Some objects such as matches, scissors, and knives can be risky and needed to be stored at height.

- Petrol cans (empty or not) should not be stored nearer to the cooking area to avoid fire.

- It is risky to have all the house materials in synthetic, e.g. bed sheets, curtains, and rugs; just to mention a few. Experienced firefighters have proved that houses that are full of synthetic materials, when subjected to an experimental fire scenario gets totally burnt down ten times quicker than houses full of cotton materials. These days the bed sheets, rugs, and curtains made from synthetic materials are always more beautiful to behold and always very attractive to the eyes than the 100 per cent cotton-made materials because the cotton-made material are not always as attractive. Therefore, people tend to go for the synthetic ones. The advice is that people should think more about their life and always choose the products made of 100 per cent cotton or the products with a higher percentage of cotton material. This information is always found on the labels of these products.

- Some people still use freezers that frost ice or blocks, which thus make them to struggle to get anything from the freezer. People, therefore, use knife to try to break the block without even bothering to switch off the freezer so that they can take the frozen food item from the freezer. This is very risky and dangerous, first the freezer is still working, taking electricity and knife (depending on its type) may conduct electricity and the risk of possible electrical shock is very high in this kind of action. The recommendation here is that one should plan ahead, thinking of possible item that may be needed from the freezer so there is no hurry about getting the food or any item out enough to tempt the person to use probably the example above. If there has been an adequate plan ahead, then the freezer be defrosted, preferably overnight, and one would be able to take out the required item without having to crack as much block or ice. With advanced technology, there are lots of reasonably priced frost-free freezers in the market, which will keep whatever item you want to freeze, and when frozen there will be no need to break through any block or ice to access it when you want to take it out.

- Cleaning of the fridge and freezer needs to be carried out very carefully to reduce the risk of an electrical shock. The recommendation is that even though the fridge or freezer is connected to the stabiliser, it is good practice to cultivate the habit of switching off the fridge or freezer before starting to clean them. It is also advisable to wear appropriate footwear while carrying out the cleaning.

- It can be risky to leave one's environment unattended, in a weedy state or in a dirty state. An environment that is not clean will breed disease causing organism. Some houses have its incinerator right in front of the house, this means that the flies that come to the incinerator may easily fly in and contaminate food or food items. Some environments have stagnated water, and in most cases, this water comes from either the bathroom or kitchen drains water should be drained completely because stagnated water will breed mosquito which causes malaria. Malaria may be fatal sometimes, so do not be careless about stagnant water. You can locally create a path for the water to drain or construct a proper drainage or gutter.

- To over work oneself is risky as continuous fatigue may cause further health issues and may lead to early death. Learn to listen to your body for any changes, especially when your body is telling you it's tired, take a break and rest. African adage says 'The life of work is longer than human life.'

- Overloading an electrical socket is also risky; some people tend to do so possibly because the location of the next available socket appears to be a little far from where they intend to use a particular electrical appliance. Most sockets have a maximum voltage that can be used for, overloading it with more voltages than its capacity may result in electrical spark or fires. Ideally, to avoid overloading a socket, junction boxes can be used although junction boxes also have maximum recommended voltage use. It is good practice to always check the recommended maximum loading of your plug or socket (it is always written somewhere on it) and adhere to such recommendations.

• Some people have the habit of forgetting to remove the plug of an electrical appliance from the switch on the wall after using it. A common example is not removing the phone charger or adapter from the charging unit even after the phone has been fully charged. The adapter is left on the plug or socket and continues to get very hot. There is a risk of possible electrical spark or fire as it is the case with other electrical appliances like TVs and Videos. Portable electrical appliances in the house should be unplugged when not in use, unless advised otherwise by the manufacturer of a particular electrical appliance. By switching off and unplugging an electrical appliance when not in use, you will be saving on electricity bills and will be minimising the risk of a possible electrical spark or fire.

• There is a popular adage which says 'dying for a call,' the question really is, is any call worth dying for. Over excitement from a good call or the shock from a bad call received while driving can be very distracting for any driver and may lead to serious accidents and hence physical deformity or death. If calls are really inevitable, earpiece should at least be worn to receive the very important calls, so that both the hands can be on the wheels to ensure that the driver is still in full control in spite of the call. But the recommendation is that for calls, that must be taken, the driver should pull aside from the road to receive such calls for safety reasons otherwise the call may as well wait till later. Your friends, relatives, and loved ones need to get to know it from you that you have not picked their calls possibly because you may be driving at the time they called. It is better safe than sorry.

- There are times in our lives that we do some things that gets us into some serious trouble that we would have wished we had not done that thing which got us into this trouble, how about thinking about things that we would remember and wished we had done them because it could have saved our lives. The use of seat belt by all passengers in a moving vehicle is often taken for granted by most people to the extent that until the road safety enforcement body catches such drivers and ask them to go and pay a stipulated amount as fine. We are talking about your life, you do not need to wait till the enforcement body is out checking for compliance, before that you use your seat belt. The recommendation is that the driver of a vehicle should always encourage everybody who are with you to wear the seat belt too. The seat belt can save life. It is also recommended that compared to an adult carrying a baby or child on their laps in a car, babies and children are to be carried about in the vehicle using a child seat or toddler-booster seat, respectively, or as required. Make sure that it is fixed in the car in accordance to the manufacturer's instructions.

- Most lamps (table or standing lamps) do have recommended watts that is fixed; it is very risky, for example, to use a 60-W bulb for a lamp recommended to use a 40-W bulb, the bulb may explode on the person trying to fix it or cause a fire. Most people just buy a lamp and believes any bulb should be okay to use with it, the recommendation here is always check for the recommended bulb's Watts which was written somewhere on the lamp to be used, or if not sure ask the retailer that you are buying it from to confirm the recommended bulb size and Watts as recommended by its manufacturer. The same principle applies for lamp holders also.

- Cleaning the ear with matchstick or any other material other than cotton bud could be risky and pose some serious dangers such as damage of the ear drum and inability to hear clearly or correctly. Cotton buds come in various sizes, and the recommendation here is to shop around to find the one suitable for your ear and use the appropriate one for yourself as an individual to avoid any unforeseeable bad occurrence.

- Sharing of sharp objects is also very risky and can pose a serious danger. There is a popular Nigerian slogan which says 'Aids no day show for face' meaning that aids does not show on the face. HIV Aids is very popular to people as one of the disease that one may risk getting if sharp objects are shared with people who have them. There are some other bacterial and viral diseases such as staph infections and hepatitis, respectively, that are not so popular but are contagious by sharing sharp objects. Our life is worth buying a personal complete kit which contains all the possible items your hairdresser needs to trim your hair. You may ask your hairdresser to make you a list of all these items and go to the salon with your own kit and insist that your own kit to be used. You may not know that a shared needle used in the salon might have just been used on an infected person and used straight away on you without been sterilised.

- River water: Most village people still drink water straight from the streams and rivers. The advice is to always boil stream or river water and allowing it to cool before drinking because of the risk of water borne diseases such as cholera. So, when you visit your family in the village for a holiday, where tap water is not yet available for use, it is worth educating them on drinking boiling water which is safe.

- Undercooked food: Undercooked food may result in food poisoning, especially meat. It is, therefore, advisable to ensure that our food is properly cooked before eating. Some food might have stayed days after being cooked, and if it has not been stored correctly then it can be very risky to eat such food, especially boiled egg, as such may cause food poisoning.

- Stacked Stools: Stools are designed to serve very simple purposes such as placing drink on it to drink from or placing plates of food to eat from. Most stools are not designed to bear the weights of a human being, some stools will even break if this is attempted. But most people tend to put stools on top of stools or chair and ask a person around to hold onto the stacked stools for support, to reach for items stacked high on the shelves or in the wardrobe or to change bulbs on the lamp-holders, this is very dangerous. Think of a typical scenario like, one of the stools mistakenly slips, and you fell off; depending on how high the stacked stools are and how deep you are in the activity you are trying to do, you will not only fall, you may fall on the person holding the stack of stools and injure this person too. Ideally, there are cheap indoor ladders, which are just two-step or a three-step ladder which should be used for such activities to avoid possible injuries like broken bones, back injury, head injury, or fractures.

- Bathroom slips and falls: Most home accidents that happens in the bathroom tend to be very serious accidents too because in many cases the people involved in such accidents suffered serious injury like broken bone or even death from a bathroom slip. The reason why this is dangerous is because the bathroom bath or shower is wet and very slippery with soapy water.

The first advice is that appropriate footwear to be worn to the bathroom as this will give a firm grip to the bathroom floor on the soapy water, which can be very slippery. Foot wear such as what is popularly called the foam or Dunlop slippers may not be a suitable footwear for a wet and slippery floor in the bathroom. Good rubber slippers with a firm sole will be more appropriate footwear to wear to the bathroom.

It is advisable that bathrooms to be fitted with handrails, this handrails will be able to provide grip to hand, in an event of a person seeming to fall. This is a good practice as it may prevent a person from smashing head against the bath or shower floor should a fall inevitably occurred, in a wet and soapy shower or bath floor. It is also advisable that the handrails be made by keeping in mind the height of the regular persons in mind. This means that about two hand rails may be necessary to be fitted in the bathrooms to accommodate the possible height requirements of the regular users so that the handrails is not too high or not too low and inaccessible when required.

Bath and shower mat may also be bought for your bathroom to provide a further firm and non-slippery bathroom floor. This is to provide an additional firm support to the appropriate footwear already worn.

- Late night eating not is not good for the body.

- House helps or maids health status: Most people are carried away by the immediate assistance they will get from the employment of a house help or maid and, therefore, do not take their time to ensure that adequate precautions have been taken so that this sought help does not leave them with a lifetime problem in the long run. A good practice will be to take the potential house help or maid to a medical check up to know their basic health status. It is very important to check and know. HIV AIDS status should be known as well as Hepatitis and any possible staph infections. This is very important, since you may not be home everyday to keep an eye on what your house help does especially when dealing with your children. You should not take this check for granted. Your house help, without your knowledge, may share sharp objects with your children, your children or even you may contact this and anything can happen from that.

Road safety is everybody's responsibility. It is the responsibility of the vehicle drivers and also of the pedestrians. The government has provided good roads, with road signs, pedestrian crossings, and traffic lights. Most people do not use the overhead pedestrian crossing thinking that it is a waste of time to do so, but imagine the serious risk in trying to cross a road about three or more lanes. It should send a message to us that it is, in fact, safer to use the provided overhead crossing. It is always good to remember the saying 'It is better to be late than never'. Traffic lights, where available, should be obeyed as it not only gives orderliness which enhances the flow of traffic but also ensures road safety, for example, it helps pedestrians to cross the road safely. People should not cross the road when the traffic light has not given signal for them to do so as they may be knocked down by a vehicle, and in this case although drivers are expected to drive carefully, it will not be the drivers fault.

Parents and adults going out with young children should be a good example to them. Our children use us as their role models and do what we do. Whenever we are at the traffic light and especially when we have young children around, even if they are not our children, and even when it appears like no vehicle is coming, always wait for the pedestrian light to go green before crossing the road.

It is also a good idea to teach the children the right and safest way to cross the road,—look right, look left, and then look right again. Be good examples to young children; do not cross the road without doing these actions as they may do what you do and may not be careful or fast enough like you, when you take such risk. When they do the same the risk and the possibility of being knocked down by a vehicle and suffering serious injuries is high, if not death.

S—Smoke Alarm

A little carelessness could result in to a fire; however, the easiest way to protect your house and family from fire is to buy and install a smoke alarm.

The sensor of a smoke alarm detects a smoke or fire, alarms, and this serves as a warning, which gives you and your family enough time to escape from a possible fire. Smoke alarm will save your life. The smoke alarm can be defined as an appliance that can detect smoke or fire at the earliest and alarms to get the people around aware hence giving them the valuable time to escape for their life.

The number of smoke alarms that may be required for each house depends on the type of the house. If it is a bungalow or flat, it is advised that the smoke alarm should be fitted in the hallway or passage. If it is a duplex or has more than one level, then it is advised that one smoke alarm should be fitted at the bottom of the stairs and one at each landing.

Offices and organisations are advised to fit smoke alarms to alert, in case a fire starts in a part of the office, the alarm will go and people will be able to escape before being hurt. Always test your alarm to ensure it is still working.

(A smoke alarm could save your life. Smoke alarm is not as expensive as some clothes we buy. To buy a smoke alarm and for free installation, please contact us via fudemfajnigltd@ymail.com.)

T—Toys

Toys can be described as the objects that are specifically made and accepted for children to play with. Most parents believe that when a product is made for babies and children, it must definitely be safe. Unfortunately, that is sometimes not the case.

Toys are good gifts for children. It gets them excited, keeps them happy. Some are educative toys, some are battery operated, some are operated by electricity, some are small in size, and some are big in size. Toys too have the possibility of becoming a dangerous thing.

Batteries of battery-operated toys may corrode without warning; this fine powder may escape, and a child may come in contact with it unaware, and this can be very dangerous. The advice here is to always check the batteries inside the toys regularly (say thrice in a month and change it earlier if required).

Electric toys can be very dangerous if it is not properly used by a child, especially when the child was not being supervised by an adult. The advice is to always check the recommended minimum age for the toys as stated on the package or box by its manufacturer. And ensure that there is always an adult around a child supervising it when the child is playing with electricity-operated toy.

Some paediatric journals have suggested that some children's development (slow development) is related to toxins in toys they play with, They may result in ear infection, allergies, etc.

When possible, the advice is to buy fabric or wooden toys because researches have also suggested that some plastic toys might have been made from cheap plastics (some cheap plastics may contain harmful chemicals that are not considered safe, especially for children).

Magnetic toys could cause choking if swallowed by a child, so make sure that magnetic toys are not bought for children who are too young to handle it especially for babies who are at the stage where they put anything that their hands can reach into their mouth.

It is a good idea to teach your children the habit of tidying up of their toys after playing with them to avoid trips and falls.

U—Uncovered Food and Bins

Leaving the food uncovered can pose a serious health and safety issue, especially in tropical regions like Africa, where there is the possibility of houseflies. Houseflies travels miles and miles, in the course of their journey, they travel through refuse dumps, incinerators, dead animals, etc. It is obvious that it is not exciting to have such fly on your food.

Always ensure the food is covered all the times.

In the market places, most foods that are cooked or uncooked are not covered to display it so that customers can notice what they are selling. This is not very good. Food items such as fish, fresh fish, and meat are often displayed in seller's trays uncovered, and flies flying on top of it. It continues to be in the same state until it is sold. Buyers need to play a part in communicating the message to the sellers by refusing to buy the uncovered displayed items and by insisting that they want an unexposed fresh one.

Bins are needed to be covered too, not many homes buy covered bins for domestic rubbish in their kitchen. The bins placed outside the house, to be collected by refuse collector, should also have covers too. For example, the leftover food placed in the bin which is uncovered will tend to invite flies, and this may cause some sort of contamination.

Please refer to the potential poison section of this book to see other possible dangers that uncovering may pose.

V—Videos and Televisions

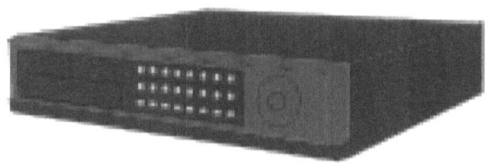

There are many electrical items commonly used in various homes, but videos and televisions appear to be the most common electrical items present in many houses. This section is focussing on the possible ways that a health and safety issue may arise from the use of these items.

Most people tend to have cultivated the habit of leaving their video and TV set on standby when going to sleep at night or even going out of the house. The danger in this is that the item is not disconnected from the electrical source. This may lead to any electrical malfunction that will affect your electrical appliance, e.g. it may blow up and stop working. A possible worse scenario could be that it may catch fire when it blows up.

The advice is that any item that has not been designed to stay on always should be switched off and unplugged when not in use, and always follows the manufacturers' instruction, whichever is applicable for your appliance.

Another good culture and a requirement by law in most advanced countries is that electrical items are subjected to a test called PAT—Portable Appliance Test. This test targets in detecting any fault in a portable electrical appliance such as kettle, TV, videos, etc. to ensure that they are safe to use at all times. There are many companies, now in Africa, which offer this service. It will further give you a peace of mind that the items are safe to use.

Please contact fudemfajnigltd@ymail.com for a PAT of the electrical items in your house.

W—Walk Safely

Having a walk is a recommended form of exercise which keeps the lungs and heart healthy and keeps the person fit.

Doctors recommend this for everybody. However, in some places, it is recommended that walks must be carried out in a safe manner. It may sound rather strange but considering your health and safety, where and when possible it is best practice to have a walk with a friend. This will ensure your security, especially if your walk is going to involve passing through a lonely and quiet place and most importantly if you are a woman. Most people will take advantage of a person when they observe that the person is alone. Walking with someone sends a message, to someone who wants to do something bad, that there is someone around to help you or help you to raise an alarm. As much as walking is good, it has to be safely done to ensure that its overall objective is not missed due to insecurity.

Choosing the right time of the day to go for a walk also matters very much. Going too early in the morning or too late at nights is not ideal for a safe walk, depending on the location where you are going for a walk.

While going for a walk, have your mobile phone with you. Store important numbers in clear languages like my dad, mummy, and my husband or wife so that a prospective helper will be able to understand and will be able to contact.

It is also a good practice to wear clothing that will make you easily spotted while having a walk. Usually, these are called high-visibility jackets and the general colour is lemon green. This is recommended because if you are walking by the road side then a driver of the vehicle can see you quickly and can take the necessary precautions if needed.

X—Xmas

Xmas is a happy season, full of activities such as cooking, putting up of the Xmas tree, visiting our loved ones, exchanging of gifts, and so on, but in this excitement accidents can easily happen.

It is very important not to display Xmas cards received from close friends close to a source of fire, e.g. a lit candle (remember, oxygen is readily available, and the card can be regarded as fuel and with a naked burning candle a fire may start).

Do not leave candle unattended or close to the Xmas tree. It has also been observed that most people begin the preparation of their Xmas food late and then they begin to rush. The advice here is to make sure that the Xmas-food preparation should begin very early to avoid last minute rush and hence a higher risk of accidents. A typical example is forgetting to blow out the wick of the stove or not properly quenching the firewood. There are records of major fire outbreak due to this carelessness.

Do not drink if you will be driving. Most people have gone to an early grave because of the excitement of the season and drunkenness.

Y—Your Medication

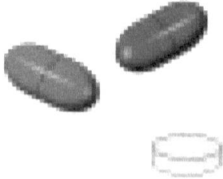

Most people tend to self-medicate, this can be dangerous, because even when we believe that the symptoms of our ailments is same as to someone we know that does not necessarily mean that the same medication given to that person will be okay for us. There are many reasons where a medication that is good for someone you know could be dangerous for you to use. For example your body weight may differ from the person's, individual allergies, diabetic state, hypertensive state, etc. Make sure you consult with your doctor before taking any medication. It is not advisable to self-medicate.

Medications should be stored above the reach of children. If medications are accessible to children, children do not know the dangers attached to this and may just help themselves to it, then it may result in possible serious health complications.

Z—Zero Tolerance to Unsafe Acts

The overall purpose of this book is to raise awareness on some health and safety issues that are often taken for granted or usually overlooked. The best approach to ensure a safe live is to adopt a zero tolerance to unsafe acts, and make sure, to the best of your ability, that the things that are often overlooked are not the cause of avoidable injuries or deaths.

It is also a good idea to inculcate this health and safety consciousness in our children so that it becomes part of their culture. Note, it may be that your little child will save your life through the health and safety consciousness which you might have instilled in them.

References

www.nhs.co.uk/handwashing—accessed on April 14, 2011 at 5.00 p.m.

www.frsc.gov.ng—accessed on April 15, 2011 at 3.00 p.m.

http://www.npf.gov.ng—accessed on April 15, 2011 at 3.00 p.m.

http://www.ghanapolice.info—accessed on May 11, 2011 at 2.00 p.m.

Clip Arts from www.openclipart.org—accessed on May 22, 2011 at 4.30 a.m.

Auto car—drawn by lmproulx

Lantern—drawn by Inky 2010

Poison bottle—drawn by jonata, liftarn, and papapishu

Video recorder—drawn by Carlos Acha Ulaje

Medication tablets—drawn by Spadassin

Mixed Xmas clip art—drawn by Inky 2010

Walking man—drawn by Jana Jakeschová andMachovka

Boy playing with toy—drawn by USDA and johnny_automatic

Pot on stove with flames—drawn by palimpsest

Simple folder photos—drawn by sarxos

Steam iron—drawn by binameusl

Fire—drawn by Valessio Soares de Brito

Gate—drawn by James Donahue and Raker Tooth

Hand washing sign—drawn by ozhank

Looking eye—drawn by paro

Person sleeping on the bed—drawn by liftarn

Plate of uncovered food—drawn by Susan Gaber and johnny_automatic

Running image—drawn by cybergedeon

Zero sign—drawn by rejon

Index

W

Fudem-Faj Nig Ltd is a wholly indigenously owned Nigeria company. It is a formally registered company that was set up as a result of recognition of the growing awareness of environmental, health and safety in Nigeria with the determination to meet such needs effectively and with guaranteed credibility. We also aim to surpass all expectation by adopting the internationally accepted standards and processes. Our email is fudemfajnigltd@ymail.com

- The director of this company; Olufunmilayo Obisesan-Fajemiseye is a registered and a recognized member of reputable national and international professional occupational and health bodies so as to ensure that high standards of work and professional competence.

Services

Fudem Nigeria Limited is involved in a range of activities to the public and private sectors; some of our activities are listed as follows:

- Delivery of quality trainings on occupational health and safety to organization/company's staffs:

Recommended Training Title(s)	Target user(s)
• Display Screen Equipment	• Users of computer & other display screens
• COSHH-Control of Substances Hazardous to Health	• Cleaners in any/all establishment, as well as other people that handles chemicals.

• First Aid (someone who will be responsible for Administering first aid person medical help arrives).	• Train appoint first aid person for schools & offices. • Training to become a first-aider.
• Manual Handling	• Stores / Warehouse Staffs. • Office where heavy files are handled.
• Moving & Assisting	• Ideal for nurses/hospital staffs who are involved with moving patient.
• Food hygiene Awareness	• Ideal for eatery/restaurants staffs.
• PPE-Personal protective equipment	• Ideal for all establishment / organization.
• Fire marshals (someone who will be responsible for safe evacuation of a building (s) in an emergency & fire drills)	• Ideal for all establishment i.e. schools, offices, churches, mosque etc.

- Delivery quality consultancy services as may be required e.g. carrying out a fire/electrical safety audit for schools, offices, hospitals etc.
- Support organizations (schools, offices, hospitals etc) to write an organizational health and safety policy that is unique to the kind of operations/activities in such establishment in order to reduce the risk.
- Carry out risk assessment for organizations and offer advice as may be required.
- General services, supplies and Occupational health and safety supplies.

www.ingramcontent.com/pod-product-compliance
Lightning Source LLC
Chambersburg PA
CBHW031251280526
45784CB00004B/1813